Piano Sol

GREAT FILM SCORES

37 THEMES BY 17 COMPOSERS

This publication is not for sale in
the E.C. and/or Australia
or New Zealand.

ISBN 0-7935-5250-8

HAL•LEONARD®
CORPORATION

7777 W. BLUEMOUND RD. P.O. BOX 13819 MILWAUKEE, WI 53213

THEMES LISTED ALPHABETICALLY BY FILM TITLE

CONTENTS

COMPOSERS FEATURED IN THIS COLLECTION

JOHN BARRY

Born in York, England on November 3, 1933, John Barry Prendergast was first introduced to the world of films as a projectionist in his father's movie theaters. After playing trumpet in a British Army band, Barry formed the John Barry Seven in 1957, with whom he performed and recorded extensively. In 1959 he began writing for film, television shows and commercials, serving for a time as the musical director and arranger for EMI Records. Even though he is equally adept at jazz, classical and popular styles, it is his melodic gift that his fans treasure. That gift is fully in evidence in two of his most beloved scores: *Dances with Wolves* and *Out of Africa*.

Selected film scores: *Dr. No* (uncredited co-composer with Monty Norman) (1962), *Born Free*** (1966), *The Lion in Winter*** (1968), *Mary, Queen of Scots** (1971), *Robin and Marian* (1976), *Body Heat* (1981), *Out of Africa*** (1985), *Dances with Wolves*** (1990), *Chaplin** (1992).

RICHARD RODNEY BENNETT

Bennett, whose mother was an accomplished pianist, was born on March 29, 1936. He began composing while still in his teens, and was educated at London's Royal Academy of Music. In 1957 he won a scholarship that allowed him to move to Paris for a two-year course of study with Pierre Boulez. When he returned to London in 1959, he began a prolific composing career, working in the jazz, classical and avant garde musical worlds. His commissions include works composed for the London Symphony Orchestra, the New York Philharmonic and the English Chamber Orchestra. Currently living in New York, he is also known as a piano accompanist and cabaret performer. *Murder on the Orient Express* shows his tongue-in-cheek approach to the music for the film, and his romantic, large-scale approach is reflected in *Nicholas and Alexandra*.

Selected film scores: *Satan Never Sleeps* (1962), *Far from the Madding Crowd** (1967), *Nicholas and Alexandra** (1971), *Murder on the Orient Express** (1974), *Tender is the Night* (1982), *Enchanted April* (1991).

GEORGES DELERUE

Born in Roubaix, France in 1925, Delerue was the son of working-class parents. Originally, he pursued music lessons to qualify for an exemption from military service, but began composing in earnest during long months of hospitalization following a spinal cord injury. After the end of the war he entered the Paris Conservatory to further his studies. His many compositions for the concert hall have won a number of awards and prizes. He once said that his concert and film music were like "two languages with the same basis." He died in California on March 20, 1992. "The Friendship Theme" from *Beaches*, presented in this folio, underscores the deep, but often turbulent, friendship between the women played by Bette Midler and Barbara Hershey.

Selected film scores: *Hiroshima, Mon Amour* (1959), *Shoot the Piano Player* (1960), *Jules and Jim* (1961), *The Pumpkin Eater* (1964), *A Man for All Seasons* (1966), *Anne of a Thousand Days** (1969), *The Day of the Dolphin** (1973), *Julia** (1977), *A Little Romance*** (1979), *Agnes of God** (1985), *Beaches* (1988).

JERRY GOLDSMITH

Jerry Goldsmith's trademark is diversity. His work is strikingly different from one motion picture to the next. He is comfortable using diverse instruments, sounds and compositional approaches, and is equally at home with symphony orchestras and the latest in electronic hardware. He was born in Los Angeles on February 10, 1929. He attended the film composition classes given by Miklós Rózsa at USC, and first composed scores for CBS radio. Graduating to television in 1955, Goldsmith wrote acclaimed scores for such hit TV series as "Thriller," "The Man from U.N.C.L.E." and "The Twilight Zone." Goldsmith's list of scores for motion pictures starts in the year 1957, and reads like an honor roll of Hollywood films. The three themes featured here show his wide compositional range–the sleazy film noire atmosphere of *Chinatown*, the excitement of *The River Wild* and the majestic, epic splendor of *Star Trek®-The Motion Picture* (which was later utilized for the "Star Trek-The Next Generation" television series).

Selected film scores: *Freud** (1963), *A Patch of Blue** (1965), *The Sand Pebbles** (1966), *Planet of the Apes** (1968), *Patton** (1970), *Papillon** (1973), *QB VII* (1974 - Television mini-series; Emmy Award), *Chinatown** (1974), *The Wind and the Lion** (1975), *The Omen*** (1976), *The Boys from Brazil** (1978), *Star Trek®-The Motion Picture** (1979), *Poltergeist** (1982), *Under Fire** (1983), *Hoosiers** (1986), *Basic Instinct** (1992), *The River Wild* (1994).

DAVE GRUSIN

Dave Grusin first established himself as a jazz pianist. He began writing scores for television and graduated to features in the late '60s. Born on June 26, 1934, he was generally identified with comedy when he was asked to do the dramatic underscore to *The Graduate*, his big break. In addition to his work in film, he has written several acclaimed compositions for symphony orchestra, and still records for GRP Records, a label he co-owned until its recent sale to MCA. The wide range of his scores (such as the three included here) show why he is so respected and in demand.

Selected film scores: *The Graduate* (1967), *Heaven Can Wait** (1978), *The Champ** (1979), *On Golden Pond** (1981), *Tootsie* (1982), *The Milagro Beanfield War*** (1988), *Havana** (1990), *The Firm** (1993).

BERNARD HERRMANN

Born on June 30, 1911, Herrmann studied the violin at an early age. But his real love was conducting, and by age twenty, he created and conducted the New Chamber Orchestra. In 1934, he went to work for CBS radio, where he served as an arranger and composer. It was his work on Orson Welles' radio shows that first brought him out to Hollywood to write the scores for *Citizen Kane* and *The Magnificent Ambersons*. He wrote memorable music for many films, and between 1955 and 1965, wrote the music to all of Alfred Hitchcock's motion pictures. He lived in London in the '70s, conducting albums of his film scores, concert works, and music by neglected composers. He died in Los Angeles on December 24, 1975, right after completing the music to *Taxi Driver*. This score was the first time he utilized jazz elements in his writing, a direction that he would have continued to explore had he lived. *Psycho* is one of the classic suspense scores of all times, and once heard is not forgotten.

Selected film scores: *Citizen Kane** (1941), *All That Money Can Buy*** (1942), *The Magnificent Ambersons* (1942), *Anna and the King of Siam** (1946), *The Ghost and Mrs. Muir* (1947), *The Seventh Voyage of Sinbad* (1958), *Psycho* (1960), *Marnie* (1964), *Obsession** (1976), *Taxi Driver** (1976).

JAMES HORNER

One of the best composers for film in Hollywood today, Horner is yet another composer that originally trained to write for the concert hall. Born on August 14, 1953, he studied at USC and UCLA. He rose to popularity with his expansive, full-orchestra score for *Star Trek*® *II: The Wrath of Khan*. Although assigned over thirty films during the '80s alone, Horner was quickly identified with the science fiction genre due to his work on *Star Trek*® *III: The Search for Spock, Krull, Cocoon* and *Aliens*. His score to *Field of Dreams* has already become a classic.

Selected film scores: *Star Trek*® *II: The Wrath of Khan* (1982), *Star Trek*® *III: The Search for Spock* (1983), *Aliens** (1986), *Willow* (1988), *Field of Dreams** (1989), *Glory* (1989), *Legends of the Fall* (1994), *Braveheart** (1995), *Apollo 13** (1995).

MAURICE JARRE

Jarre was born in Lyons, France on September 13, 1924. He wrote concert music and film scores in France when he received a call from director David Lean to write the score to *Lawrence of Arabia*. The incredible success of this score catapulted Jarre to worldwide fame and many assignments. In addition to his orchestral scores, Jarre has become renowned for his electronic scores for such films as *Witness*. Both scores to *Ghost* and *Fatal Attraction* have become cult classics.

Selected film scores: *Lawrence of Arabia*** (1962), *Doctor Zhivago*** (1965), *Ryan's Daughter* (1970), *Mohammed, Messenger of God** (1974), *The Tin Drum* (1979), *A Passage to India*** (1984), *Witness** (1984), *Fatal Attraction* (1987), *Gorillas in the Mist** (1988), *Ghost** (1990).

HENRY MANCINI

Mancini was born on April 16, 1924 in Cleveland, Ohio. His father taught him to play the flute, and young Henry learned to write arrangements from Max Adkins in Pittsburgh, Pennsylvania. After service in World War II, Mancini joined the Glenn Miller Orchestra as arranger and pianist. In 1951, he joined the composing staff of Universal Pictures where he remained until 1958. His break came when producer Blake Edwards asked him to write the music for the television show "Peter Gunn." Mancini recorded the music for an album, and the album became a best-seller. *Breakfast at Tiffany's* won for Mancini his first of many Oscars for Best Score or Song. A successful composer of film scores (his descriptive "Baby Elephant Walk" not only enhanced the action in the film, but was a million-selling record), concert music and pop songs, Mancini also became a concert conductor and TV personality. He was completing the score for the Broadway show *Victor/Victoria* when he died on June 14, 1994 in Los Angeles.

Selected film scores: *The Glenn Miller Story** (co-composer - 1954), *Breakfast at Tiffany's*** (1961), *Days of Wine and Roses* (1962), *Hatari!* (1962), *The Pink Panther** (1964), *Charade* (1964), *Sunflower** (1969), *The Molly Maguires* (1970), *10** (1979), *Victor/Victoria*** (1984), *The Glass Menagerie* (1987).

ENNIO MORRICONE

One of the most prolific composers in film music history, Morricone was born in Rome on October 11, 1928. His earliest scores were Italian light comedies and costume pictures, where Morricone learned to write simple, memorable themes. His themes for such films as *A Fistful of Dollars, For a Few Dollars More* and *The Good, the Bad and the Ugly* became best-selling records. He writes music for films produced all over the world. *The Mission, The Untouchables* and the poetic *Cinema Paradiso* are three of his most beloved scores.

Selected film scores: *A Fistful of Dollars* (1964), *For a Few Dollars More* (1965), *The Good, the Bad and the Ugly* (1966), *Once Upon a Time in the West* (1969), *Exorcist II: The Heretic* (1977), *Days of Heaven** (1978), *Once Upon a Time in America* (1985), *The Mission** (1986), *The Untouchables** (1987), *Cinema Paradiso* (1989).

ALEX NORTH

Yet another composer who started writing music for the ballet and concert hall, North was born in Chester, Pennsylvania on December 4, 1910. Attending the Curtis Institute and the Juilliard School of Music, he went to Russia and became a telegraph operator, but was soon homesick, as he later said, for American jazz. Upon his return, he studied composition with Aaron Copland, Ernst Toch and Silvestre Revueltas. He composed music for the stage version of *A Streetcar Named Desire*, and director Elia Kazan insisted that he compose the music for the film version. North's score was acclaimed, and he was active as a composer for motion pictures until his death on September 8, 1991. Able to work in many genres, he often was called to write music for spectacles, of which *Spartacus* was one of his best. In 1985, North was the first composer to receive an honorary Academy Award for lifetime achievement.

Selected film scores: *A Streetcar Named Desire** (1951), *Death of a Salesman** (1951), *Viva Zapata!** (1952), *The Rose Tattoo** (1955), *The Rainmaker** (1956), *Spartacus** (1960), *Cleopatra** (1963), *The Agony and the Ecstasy** (1965), *Shanks** (1974), *Bite the Bullet** (1975), *Dragonslayer** (1981), *Under the Volcano** (1984).

NINO ROTA

Born in Milan, Italy on December 31, 1911, Rota was a prodigy in music, composing large-scale orchestral works, and even an opera, while he was still in his teens. He studied at the Milan Conservatory with Alfredo Casella, and the Curtis Institute of Music in the United States. His professional relationships with the great Italian directors such as Federico Fellini (*Amarcord, 8 1/2, La dolce vita*), Luchino Visconti (*The Leopard*), and Franco Zeffirelli *(Romeo and Juliet)* allowed him to write some of the finest film music ever composed. Perhaps his greatest success was the music for the Francis Ford Coppola *Godfather* trilogy. Rota died in Rome on April 10, 1979.

Selected film scores: *I Vitelloni* (1953), *La Strada* (1954), *War and Peace* (1956), *Nights of Cabiria* (1957), *La dolce vita* (1960), *Rocco and His Brothers* (1960), *8 1/2* (1963), *The Leopard* (1963), *Juliet of the Spirits* (1965), *Romeo and Juliet* (1968), *The Godfather* (1972), *The Godfather, Part II*** (co-composed with Carmine Coppola) (1974), *The Godfather, Part III* (1990).

MIKLÓS RÓZSA

Like other Hungarian composers as Bela Bartok and Zoltan Kodaly, Rózsa's music is imbued with the Folk music of his native land. Born in Budapest, Hungary on April 18, 1907, Rózsa studied the violin as a child, later taking up the piano. Formal music training continued in Leipzig in the late '20s, and in 1932, Rózsa settled in Paris. As his reputation as a concert composer grew, he began writing background music for documentaries and newsreels. Eventually he attracted the attention of producer Alexander Korda, and began his film score career in earnest in the late '30s in England. Moving to Hollywood in 1940, his scores for Paramount, Selznick and MGM became instant classics. *Spellbound*, in particular, was tremendously popular, featuring the unusual instrument, the theramin. Rózsa taught for many years at USC, conducted many concerts at the Hollywood Bowl, and continued his composition of concert music almost until his death in 1995.

Selected film scores: *The Thief of Baghdad** (1940), *Jungle Book** (1942), *Double Indemnity** (1944), *The Lost Weekend** (1945), *Spellbound*** (1945), *The Killers** (1946), *A Double Life*** (1947), *Quo Vadis** (1951), *Ivanhoe** (1952), *Julius Caesar** (1953), *Ben Hur*** (1959), *El Cid** (1961), *Time after Time* (1979).

ALAN SILVESTRI

Born in New York on March 20, 1950, Silvestri was raised in Teaneck, New Jersey. He attended Berklee College and played in rock bands upon graduation. He wrote the music for the television show "CHIPS," and helped out writing some cues for the film *Romancing the Stone*. The director of the film was so impressed, he asked Silvestri to write the entire score. The director was Robert Zemeckis (who later made *Back to the Future* and *Forrest Gump*), and the score launched Silvestri's career.

Selected film scores: *Romancing the Stone* (1984), *Back to the Future* trilogy (1985, 1989, 1990), *Who Framed Roger Rabbit?* (1988), *The Abyss* (1989), *Grumpy Old Men* (1993), *Forrest Gump* (1994).

VANGELIS (Vangelis Odyssey Papathanoussiou)

Born in Valos, Greece on March 29, 1943, Vangelis was a child prodigy, performing publicly on the piano at the age of six. He moved to France and was a member of the group Aphrodite's Child with vocalist Demis Rousos. When the group disbanded, Vangelis moved to London. His recordings with Jon Anderson of the group Yes were praised in music magazines and sold well. Vangelis' score for *Chariots of Fire* made him an international star, and the soundtrack album continues to be a best-seller.

Selected film scores: *Chariots of Fire*** (1981), *Blade Runner* (1982), *Missing* (1982), *The Bounty* (1984), *1492: Conquest of Paradise* (1992).

JOHN WILLIAMS

After years of being out of fashion, the lush, romantic, sweeping full-orchestral score made a major comeback in John Towner Williams' score for the blockbuster *Star Wars*. Pretty good for a classically trained pianist who first became known as a jazz player and arranger. Williams was born in Flushing, New York on February 8, 1932, the son of Johnny Williams, for years a drummer on staff at CBS radio. Besides playing jazz piano, Williams played in many studio orchestras, and eventually broke into series television in the late '50s. After years of scoring musicals, light comedies and disaster movies, *Star Wars* made Williams the number one composer in Hollywood. Its soundtrack album became the biggest-selling symphonic film score in history. Such themes as "E.T. (The Extra-Terrestrial)," "Raiders March," and the theme from *Schindler' List* are staples at pops concerts all over the world. For many years, Williams conducted the Boston Pops, and became a familiar face via the orchestra's television broadcasts. He is the composer of several concert works, including symphonies, concertos and fanfares.

Selected film scores: (# indicates nomination for Best Song Score Adaptation category) *Goodbye, Mr. Chips*#** (1969), *The Reivers** (1970), *Fiddler on the Roof*#** (1971), *Images** (1972), *The Poseidon Adventure** (1972), *The Towering Inferno** (1974), *Jaws*** (1975), *Star Wars*** (1976), *Close Encounters of the Third Kind** (1977), *Superman** (1978), *The Empire Strikes Back** (1980), *Indiana Jones* trilogy* (1981, 1984, 1989), *E.T. (The Extra-Terrestrial)*** (1982), *Return of the Jedi** (1983), *Born on the Fourth of July** (1989), *JFK** (1991), *Schindler's List*** (1993).

HANS ZIMMER

A pioneer in the use of electronic instruments in film scoring, Zimmer began his career in Europe. Born on September 12, 1957 in Frankfurt, Germany, Zimmer played the piano from the age of three. He moved to London during the '70s, played in bands and wrote commercials. He worked on several scores with the British composer Stanley Myers, and eventually broke into U.S. series televisions with his scores for "Miami Vice." One of his most popular scores was for the poignant *Driving Miss Daisy*.

Selected film scores: *My Beautiful Laundrette* (1985), *Rain Man** (1988), *Driving Miss Daisy* (1989), *Days of Thunder* (1990), *Thelma and Louise* (1991), *True Romance* (1993), *The Lion King*** (1994), *The Fan* (1995).

THE JOHN DUNBAR THEME
from DANCES WITH WOLVES

By JOHN BARRY

Moderately

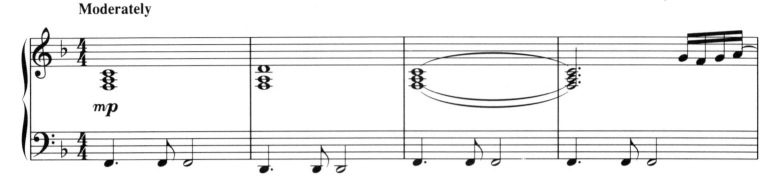

To Coda $\oplus$

(End opt. 8va)

12

D.S. al Coda

CODA

LOVE THEME FROM OUT OF AFRICA
(THE MUSIC OF GOODBYE)
from OUT OF AFRICA

Music by JOHN BARRY
Words by ALAN and MARILYN BERGMAN

MCA music publishing

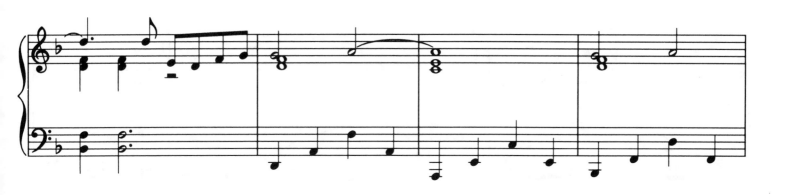

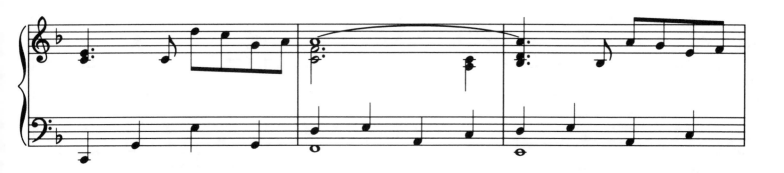

NICHOLAS AND ALEXANDRA
Theme from NICHOLAS AND ALEXANDRA

By RICHARD RODNEY BENNETT

Moderate, flowing

MURDER ON THE ORIENT EXPRESS
from the Paramount Motion Picture MURDER ON THE ORIENT EXPRESS

Music by
RICHARD RODNEY BENNETT

Moderately

THE FRIENDSHIP THEME

from Touchstone Pictures' BEACHES

Music by
GEORGES DELERUE

Gently Flowing

mp

With pedal

CHINATOWN
from the Paramount Motion Picture CHINATOWN

Music by
JERRY GOLDSMITH

Slowly

GALE'S THEME
(MAIN TITLE)
from THE RIVER WILD

By JERRY GOLDSMITH

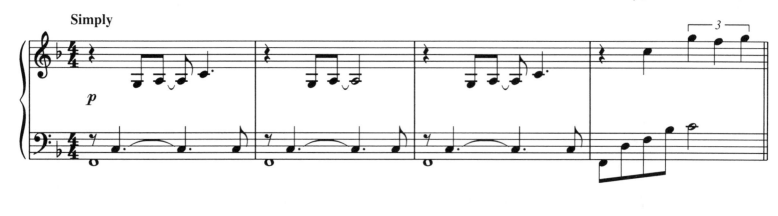

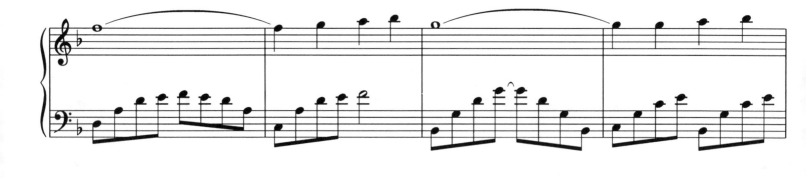

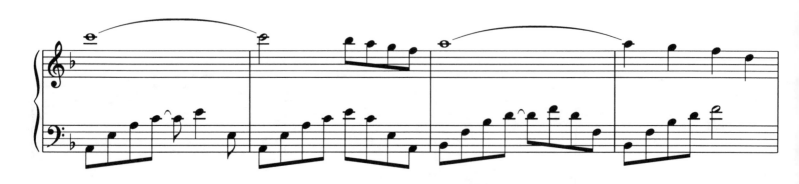

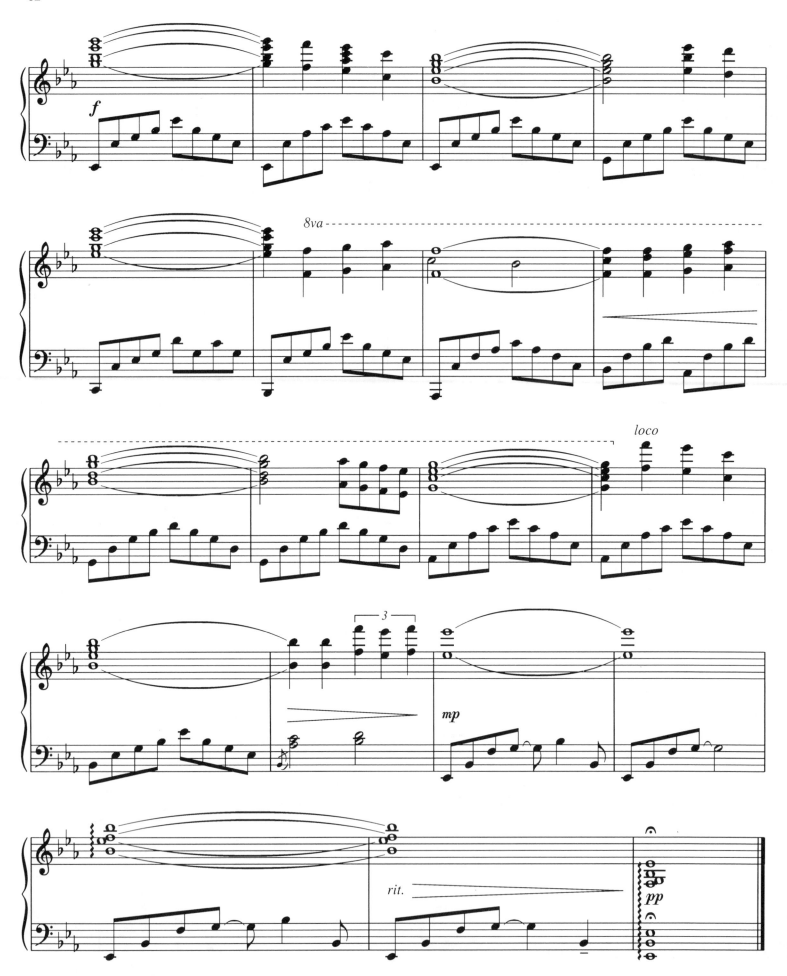

STAR TREK® - THE MOTION PICTURE
Theme from the Paramount Picture STAR TREK

Music by
JERRY GOLDSMITH

Slowly

Power Rock shuffle

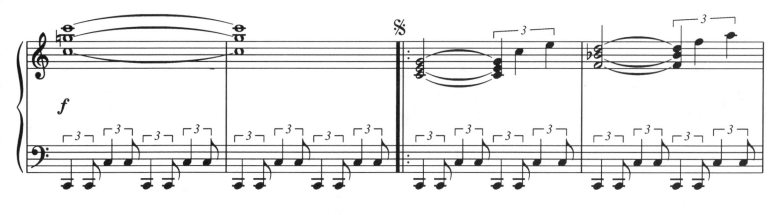

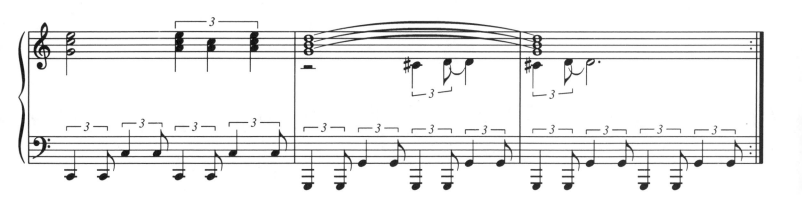

THE FIRM - MAIN TITLE
from the Paramount Motion Picture THE FIRM

By DAVE GRUSIN

Moderately, with a steady pulse

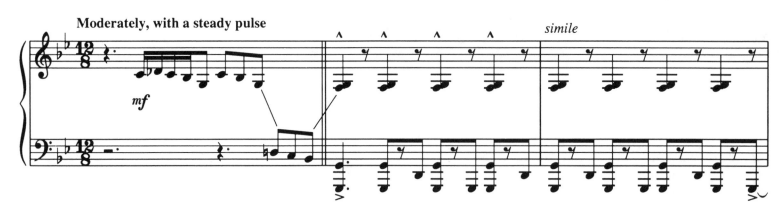

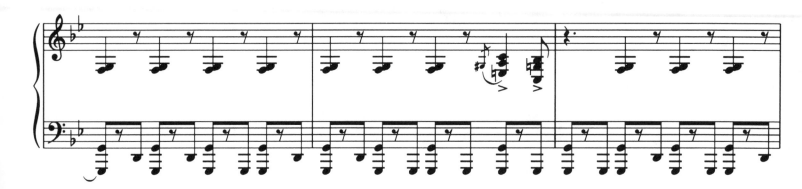

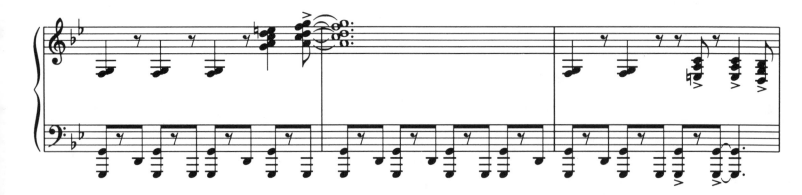

42

ON GOLDEN POND
Main Theme from ON GOLDEN POND

Music by
DAVE GRUSIN

*Not fast and somewhat freely

44

46

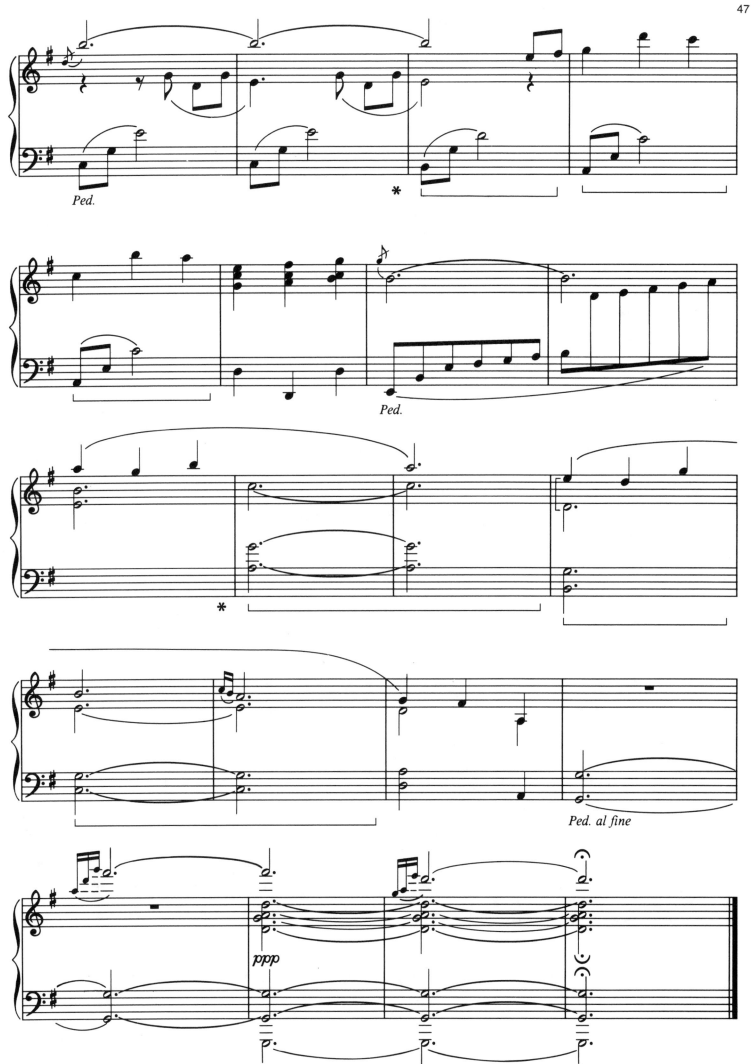

HEAVEN CAN WAIT
(Love Theme)
from the Paramount Motion Picture HEAVEN CAN WAIT

Music by DAVE GRUSIN

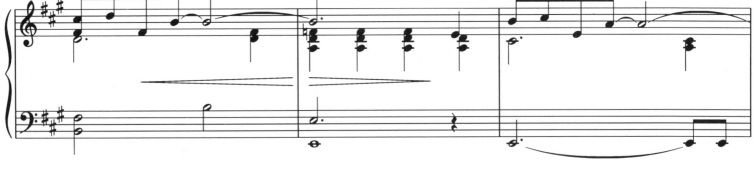

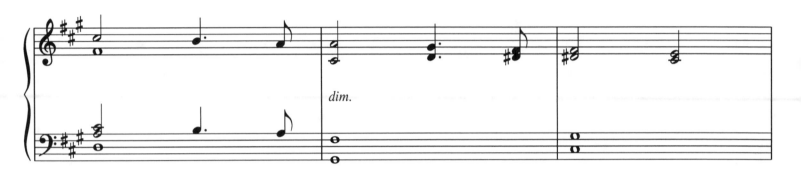

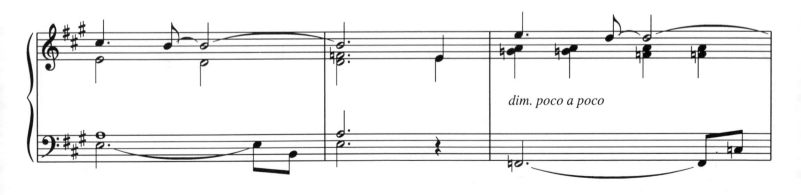

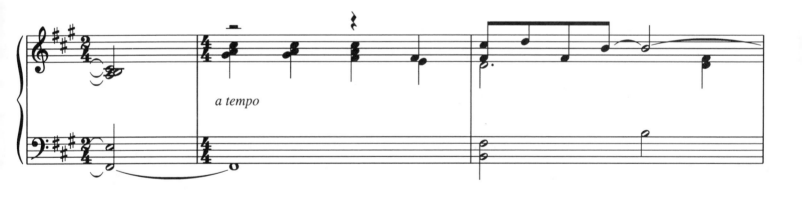

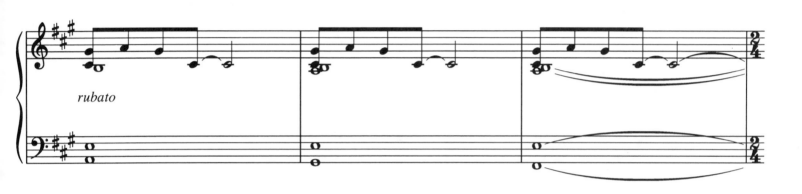

PSYCHO
(Prelude)
Theme from the Paramount Picture PSYCHO

Music by
BERNARD HERRMANN

Poco agitato

TAXI DRIVER
(Theme)
from TAXI DRIVER

By BERNARD HERRMANN

Rubato, expressivo (slow feeling)

THE WRATH OF KAHN
(Theme from Star Trek®II)
from the Paramount Motion Picture STAR TREK II: THE WRATH OF KAHN

Music by ALEXANDER COURAGE
and JAMES HORNER

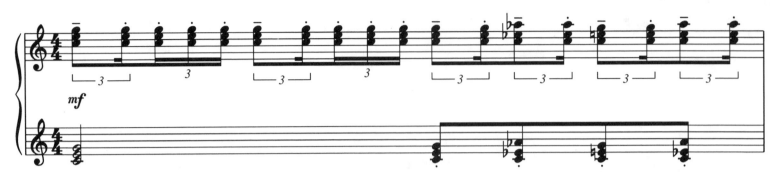

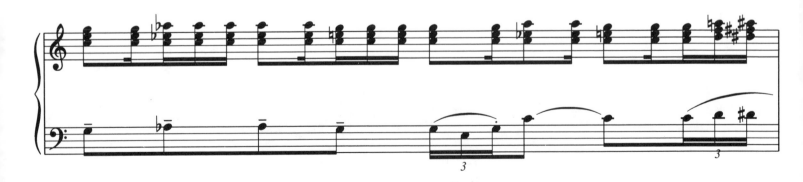

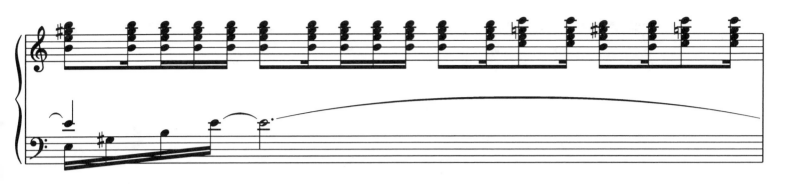

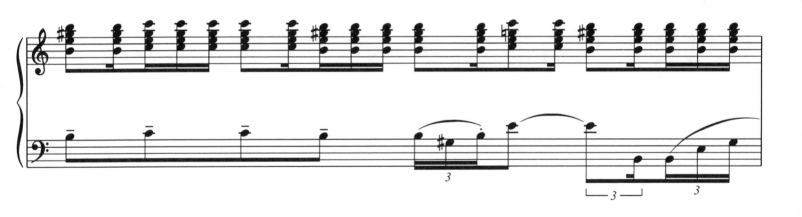

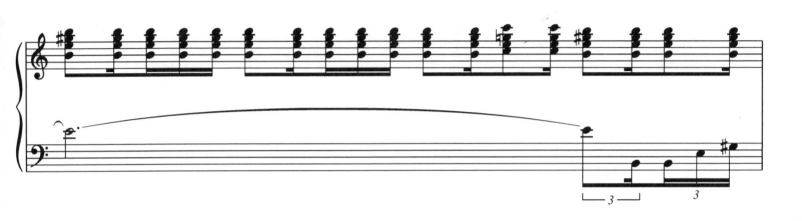

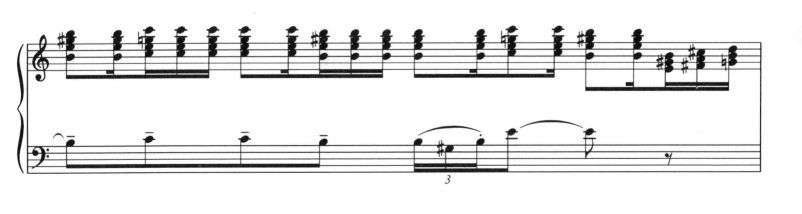

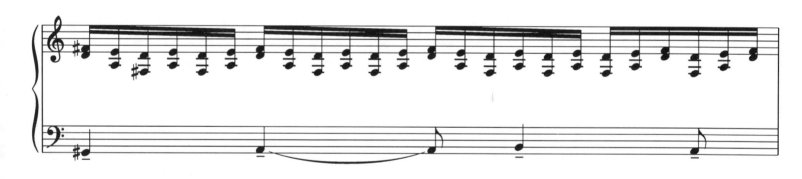

Main Theme

64

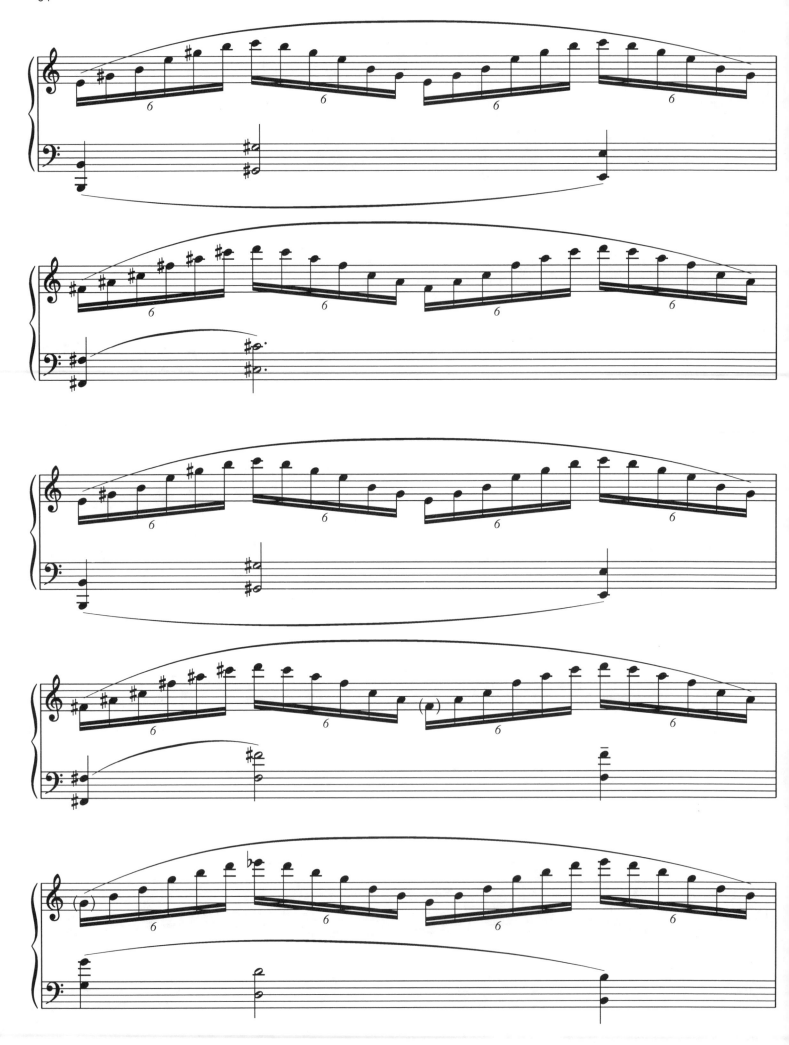

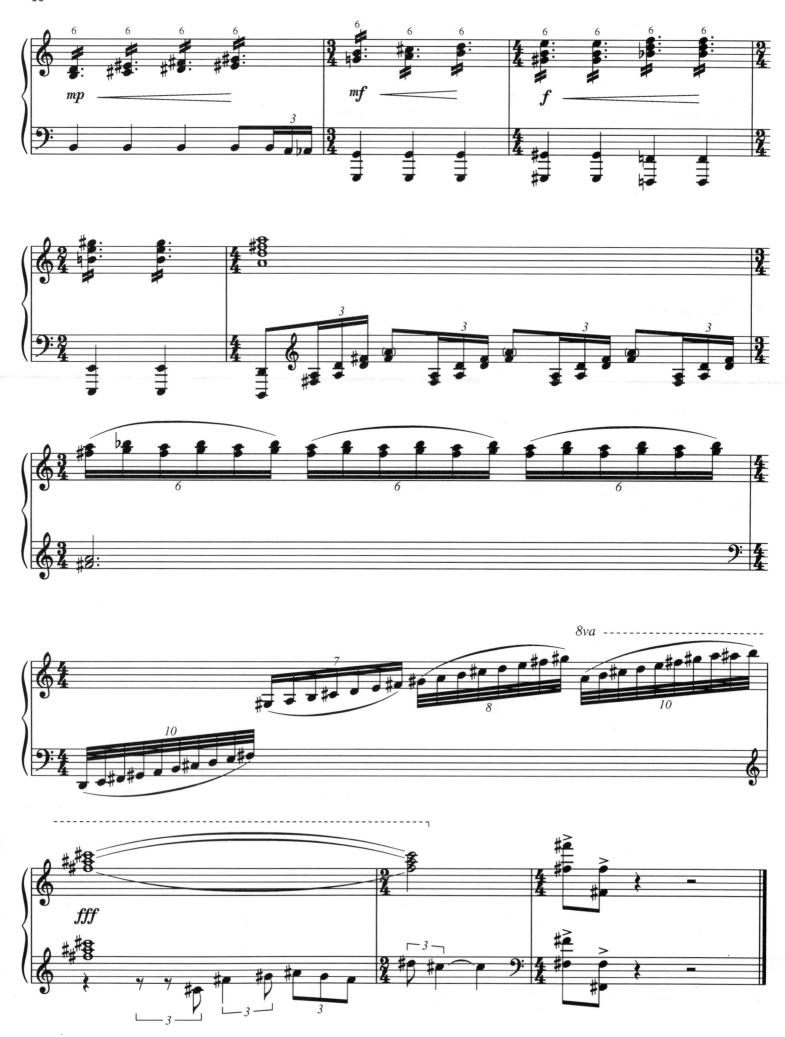

THE SEARCH FOR SPOCK

(Theme from Star Trek®III)
from the Paramount Motion Picture STAR TREK III: THE SEARCH FOR SPOCK

Music by
JAMES HORNER

8vb--

THEME FROM "FATAL ATTRACTION"
from the Paramount Motion Picture FATAL ATTRACTION

Music by
MAURICE JARRE

Slowly

GHOST
Theme from the Paramount Motion Picture GHOST

By MAURICE JARRE

Expressively

Very slowly and mysteriously

THEME FROM "LAWRENCE OF ARABIA"

from LAWRENCE OF ARABIA

By MAURICE JARRE

80

BREAKFAST AT TIFFANY'S
Theme from the Paramount Picture BREAKFAST AT TIFFANY'S

Music by
HENRY MANCINI

Moderately, with expression

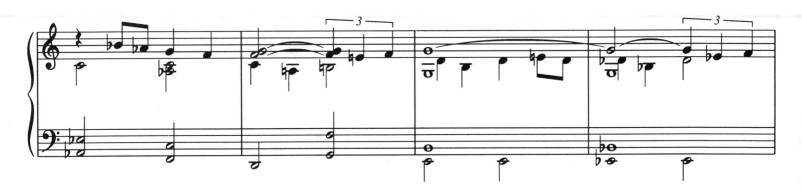

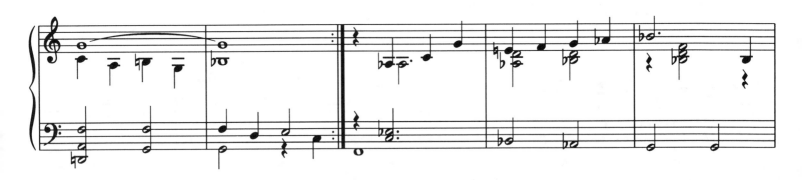

To Coda ⊕

D.C. al Coda

CODA
⊕

rall.

BABY ELEPHANT WALK
from the Paramount Picture HATARI!

By HENRY MANCINI

Moderately slow and steady

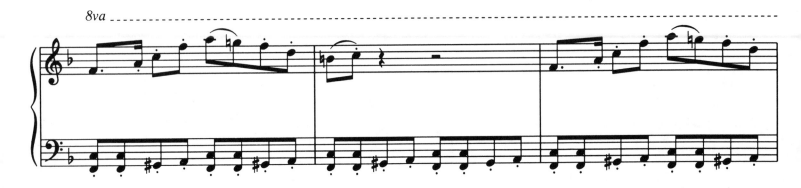

CINEMA PARADISO

from CINEMA PARADISO

Music by
ENNIO MORRICONE

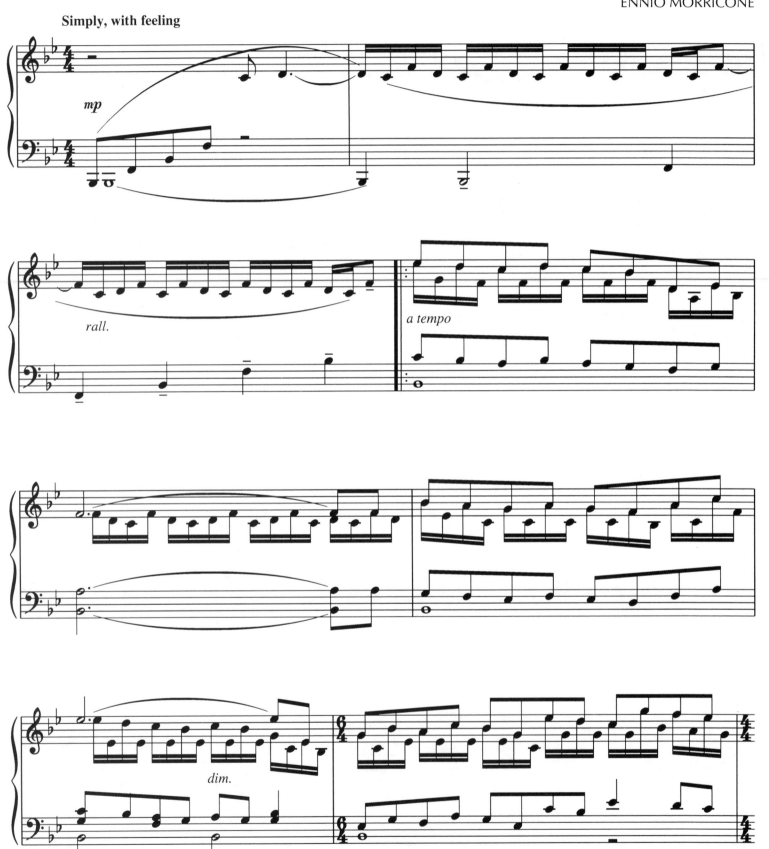

RIVER
from the Motion Picture THE MISSION

Music by
ENNIO MORRICONE

THE UNTOUCHABLES - MAIN TITLE

from the Paramount Motion Picture THE UNTOUCHABLES

Words and Music by
ENNIO MORRICONE

Maestoso

D.S. al Coda

CODA

Allargando

SPARTACUS - LOVE THEME
from the Universal - International Picture Release SPARTACUS

By ALEX NORTH

Moderato

LA DOLCE VITA
Theme from the film LA DOLCE VITA

Music by NINO ROTA
Lyrics by DINO VERDE

Moderato

AMARCORD
Theme from the film AMARCORD

By NINO ROTA

Ritmo Moderato

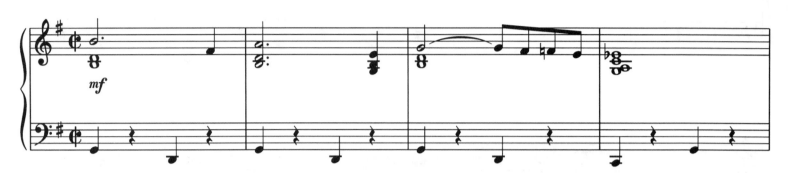

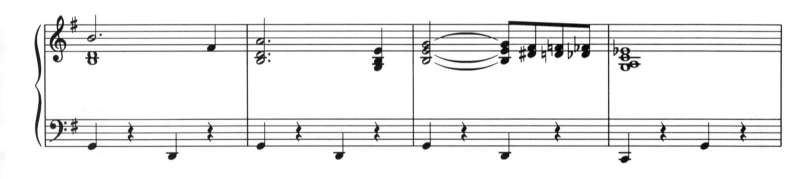

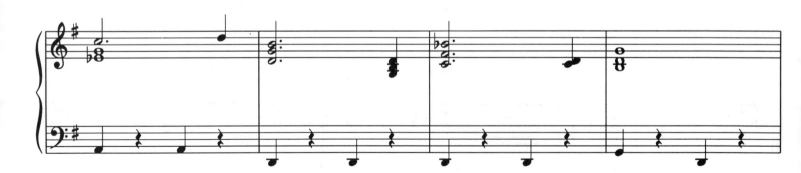

LA PASSERELLA DI ADDIO

Theme from the film 8 1/2

Music by NINO ROTA

Allegro moderato

107

rall.

THE GODFATHER
(LOVE THEME)
from the Paramount Picture THE GODFATHER

By NINO ROTA

Slowly and expressively

GODFATHER II
Theme from the Paramount Picture GODFATHER II

By NINO ROTA

Andante

SPELLBOUND
from SPELLBOUND

Words by MACK DAVID
Music by MIKLÓS RÓZSA

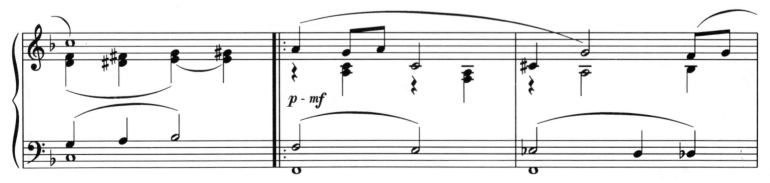

CHARIOTS OF FIRE
from CHARIOTS OF FIRE

Music by
VANGELIS

Moderately

BACK TO THE FUTURE
from the Universal Motion Picture BACK TO THE FUTURE

By ALAN SILVESTRI

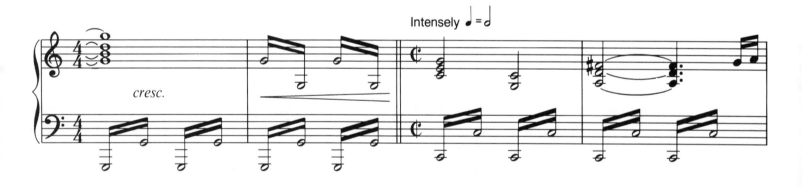

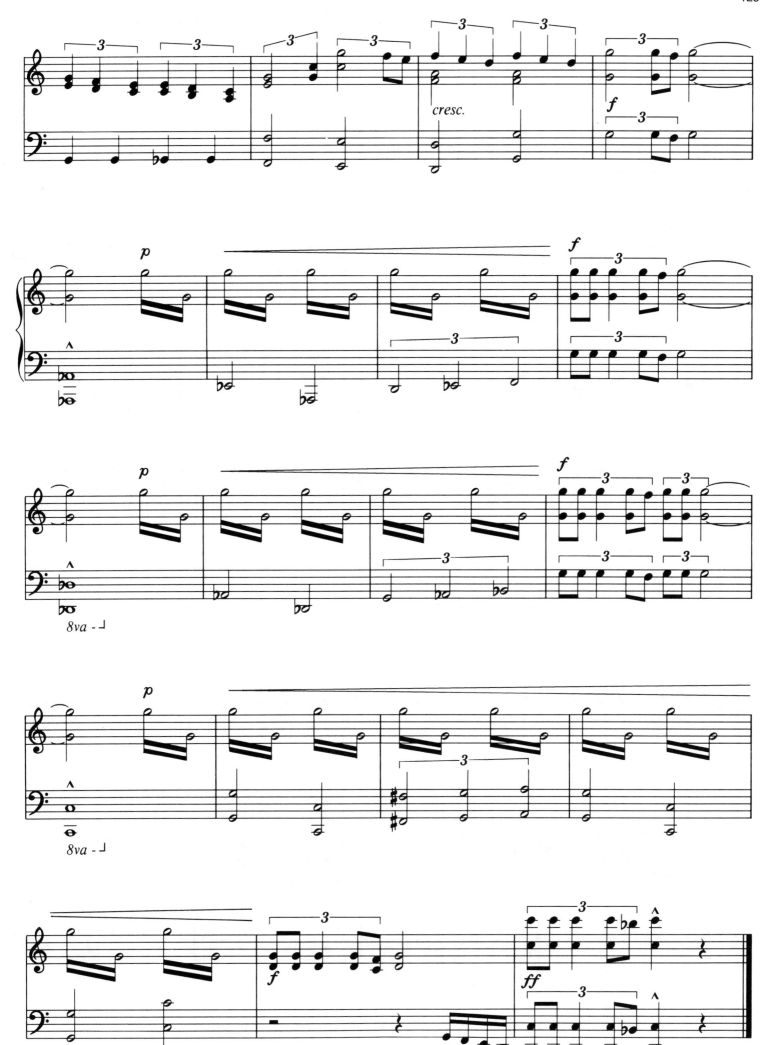

FORREST GUMP - MAIN TITLE
(FEATHER THEME)
from the Paramount Motion Picture FORREST GUMP

Music by
ALAN SILVESTRI

Sweetly

8va

f

(lightly)

THEME FROM "SCHINDLER'S LIST"
from the Universal Motion Picture SCHINDLER'S LIST

Composed by
JOHN WILLIAMS

MCA music publishing

RAIDERS MARCH
from the Paramount Motion Picture RAIDERS OF THE LOST ARK

By JOHN WILLIAMS

March tempo

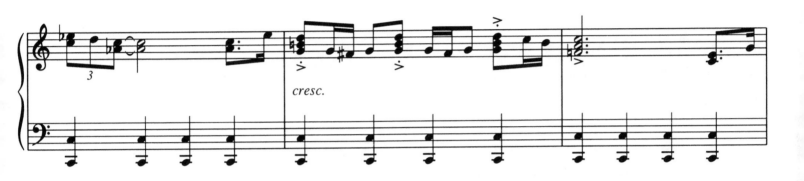

sim.

THEME FROM E.T.
(THE EXTRA-TERRESTRIAL)
from the Universal Picture E.T. (THE EXTRA-TERRESTRIAL)

Music by
JOHN WILLIAMS

MCA music publishing

DRIVING MISS DAISY
from DRIVING MISS DAISY

By HANS ZIMMER

Moderately

144